THE ULTIMATE GUIDE FOR
EMPLOYEE SUCCESS

GROW YOUR PAYCHECK

"LEARN EFFECTIVE STRATEGIES TO UPLIFT YOUR PROFESSIONAL GROWTH, CREDIBILITY, WORTHINESS AND BECOME THE MOST DEPENDABLE EMPLOYEE"

Author
Advocate Swapnil Modi
M.B.A. (HR) and LL.B. (Gold Medalist)

Warning

Table of Contents

Acknowledgements

This book is my sincere endeavor to put in one place all the hacks of scaling up one's professional career, though compiling vast information on these topics is an impossible task but I have put in my reasonable best efforts to incorporate essential elements required to level up your career.

I am sincerely thankful to the following people who played an important role by taking me ahead in the journey of writing this book:

I shall always be grateful to Advocate Krishna S., the one who inspired me to write this book, and for being my first reader and giving me continuous constructive feedback in completing this book. I remain deeply obliged to her.

Thank you, thank you, thank you to my designer, Marmie S., for your creative vision in designing my book cover.

My thanks also go out to my mentors, my management team for their unmatched support, without your support I would have not reached to this level.

I am also acutely thankful to my loving mother Kashmira Chotubhai Rakhashia and my younger brother Vicky Prafulkumar Modi for their constant love and support, along with the blessings of my father late Shri. Prafulkumar Natwarlal Modi.

Also, my friends without you, my life is incomplete.

Thank you everyone for always believing in me and giving me your blessings and enormous love. I am blessed to have you all in my life.

Suggestions are most welcome from my readers and nothing in this book is meant in any way to offend anyone expressly or impliedly.

And countless thanks to the ALMIGHTY GOD, for always backing me up and making things possible with your unconditional support.

I take this opportunity to communicate with all working professionals and give them a simple message:

****

"Work not only to survive, but work to gain knowledge."

"Work not only for the sake of working, but work with complete dedication."

"Work not only to pay your dues, but work to grow in your professional career."

****

Prologue

Admit it, you must have thought that you are underpaid or you should get paid a little higher for all the work you are currently doing. If yes, then have you thought of the different possibilities to increase your performance to grow your paycheck? And if you have mentally accepted your existing paycheck, then that's all you'd get paid and you won't to get paid any higher. Some people are perfectly happy staying in the same role for their entire career, and they don't want to advance up the career ladder. Everybody wants to move up but only a few are able to step-up, do you know why? It's a matter of personal preference, and if you are happy with current scenario even if your paycheck is low but if you mentally accepted it then you won't give any efforts to change it. It is completely your choice; if you think it for once then you'd be bombarded with lots of interconnected questions and thoughts related to that one point which you had consciously thought of. *What if I say:* **YES! You can** "**GROW YOUR PAYCHECK**." *How does that sound?*

I have encountered many professionals in my over 15 years of corporate experience and one thing I can say that every individual is not a born entrepreneur, off-course with no offence to those who are. However, I had noticed that there are huge number of professionals who either love their work or they have developed their comfort zone and don't wish to break their own created limitations and pretend to love their work.

There could be many reasons, and few of those are:

- ✓ They don't wish to take any risk. (Often people afraid of taking new challenges.)
- ✓ They like to continue the way they are operating and remain in their comfort zone.
- ✓ They have built a rapport in their organization over a period of time which they don't want to lose. After all it takes a decent time to build trust.

- ✓ They don't wish to encash their goodwill and join new employer and start building a new rapport.
- ✓ They have a family commitment that carries more priority than taking risk.
- ✓ They have financial commitments and don't wish to put all of those at a *STAKE* by entering into entrepreneurship.

What's in it for me?

After reading this book and implementing these strategies in your work, you will be able to improve your professional stand, create worthiness, uplift your growth by adding more value to your organization and become most dependable employee. The steps that I have narrated in this book are in the form of chapters that will make you to re-think about your existing stand in your organization, simultaneously you should also see a glimpse of your upcoming role in your organization. Remember, first and foremost step is, "*Visualize*" and give yourself a command regularly and be absolute confident that you've acquired that new position in your organization. Once, you have envisaged yourself then, you should follow your plan of action. Ensure that all of your actions are going in the correct direction and you will achieve your goals in the very near future.

Why?

Why do you want to GROW YOUR PAYCHECK? If you want to stay in your current job, working for your present employer, you can ask for a pay raise at work or speak up for yourself. Asking for a hike in salary is the also one of the way to get a higher amount of pay but before asking for pay raise, you must ask yourself following questions:

i) On what all grounds I am asking for the rate increase?

ii) Am I asking for just the industry standard rate increase which shall be applicable to other team members?

iii) Am I asking for a decent salary increase that is beyond industry standards?

iv) Is it equally proportional against the work I have delivered in previous year?

v) What additional values I have added to the organization?

vi) Have I delivered extra work other than my expected roles/duties in previous year? and few alike questions.

The idea is not to demoralize you or to stop you from asking for pay increase, but eventually this will help you stand confident when you speak for yourself as you have all your achievements and outcomes of your previous year handy. You have also shown your dedication towards your organization and set a benchmark for yourself. Hence, if you are able to effectively present your efforts, work and previous year's achievements then undoubtedly you'd receive decent hike. However, if you aren't mentally prepared for all of these, then it will be a nightmare for you to get decent hike on your salary. You must get what you deserve either its appreciation or promotion. It's a simple theory of happy living, if you're happy that means you are satisfied. I have seen many hardworking team members in corporate organizations who don't get decent hike due to their inability to show-cast their efforts v/s there are also 5% people in every organization who work smart and portrait their work in more effective manner to get recognition from the management and they are able to seek decent raise in their salary.

Note down all of those additional responsibilities, accountabilities that you undertook, and all of these should be over and above your expected roles & responsibilities.

Write down your extra work

✓ Do the assessment of your current annual work for which you are getting paid. Note down all of your key responsibilities in the below given writing space:

_____

_____

_____

_____

_____

_____

_____

✓ It's really a noticeable point; pen-down of your additional values that have boosted your organization's growth in any manner in the below given space.

_____

_____

_____

_____

_____

_____

_____

_____

_____

_____

_____

_____

Write down your extra initiatives

✓ All those initiatives that you took in previous year (again this should be over and above your regular job duties & responsibilities.)

Initiatives:

_____

_____

_____

_____

_____

_____

_____

_____

_____

_____

_____

✓ Extra efforts which you have given to your team & team members to make them achieve their task and their targets.

Extra efforts:

_____

_____

_____

_____

_____

_____

_____

_____

_____

_____

_____

_____

_____

✓ Any additional task you undertook involving the process improvement or which had increased the productivity of your team.

Additional task:

_____

_____

_____

_____

_____

_____

_____

_____

_____

_____

_____

_____

_____

Be prepared to justify the number you are asking in your salary review:

Before jumping into asking for a pay raise and presenting your expectations, you must ask yourself:

✓ Do you have enough experience for pay raise? Are you eligible for a salary review?

❖ Usually, salary review takes place annually in corporates or half-yearly depending upon organizations' structure. Check this first and if you still have any doubts then ask your immediate supervisor.

- ✓ Have you talked about it with your immediate supervisor?

  - ❖ Discuss about compensation with your immediate supervisor first and tell him your expectation based upon your work delivered. Discuss with him thoroughly.

- ✓ Is your performance worth for getting hike in your pay raise?

  - ❖ If you have achieved your assigned annual targets then you can confidently ask for a good pay raise, however; if you are falling short in achieving your targets then you won't be in a position to demand a good raise.

✓ Have you learned new skills or completed additional training in comparison to others for getting hike in your pay raise?

❖ If you have achieved the new skills that makes you more valuable as an employee than others which had helped in growth of organization than you must demand a raise.

How?

Instead of thinking about your past and getting demotivated with the feeling of underpaid and spoiling your mood. *"Invest..... Invest.... Invest..."* that same time in upgrading your skills, improving your current position, and getting prepared for future & upcoming challenges and requirements. These new skills and new learning along with a positive state of mind will last forever if practiced regularly. Remember, the mistakes and failures of the past shouldn't hurt you because it's over and you can't change it. The sooner you accept it, the sooner you will overcome negative emotions and grow a positive mindset. Always learn lesson from your past and don't repeat it.

Let's see the some of the proven steps that can help you grow in your organization.

By taking extra accountability

Be accountable and increase your moral obligation by fulfilling your commitments. Set a higher expectation and understand your responsibilities. Get a little more casual and balance your time and work to perform better. Once when you find yourself accountable, you perform the work more efficiently and effectively and you will try to take extra responsibility of additional task other than your assigned ones. Accountability makes you more responsible, progressive and allows you to measure your success. This is the only way to push yourself towards a better you and being a responsible employee by giving the best output to your organization.

By panoramic growth in the personality:

While working in an organization, you have to go through different situation which is against your set of belief. So for the growth of the organization, you need to accept those situations which are beneficial for the organization and should go outside from your comfort zone.

By showing your positive approach & attitude towards accepting new challenges

Show your positive approach & attitude towards accepting new challenge in front of your management. The first step is to think positive and response positively. Use more complex vocabulary, it can really change the way you speak and write. Learn to manage stress and situation of new challenges without any fear. Instead of using words such as '*problem*' or '*issue*' use words like '*situation*' and accept every situation that arrives in organization. Second step is reactions, instead of saying '*it's tough*' and '*I can't*' use '*it's challenging but interesting*' and '*I can & I will*'. It wouldn't make the task easier but yes, it will make you stronger and keep you focused on your work. It will surely help you to come out from your comfort zone and encourage you to update your skills (if required) to meet the demand of the changing scenario. Remember, you've already **WON** half of the battle by accepting the new challenge, because confronting a challenge will spark greater change within yourself. Now it's the time to give maximum output from minimum input to the organization and get rewarded.

By learning required skills to complete the task undertaken by you

Express your interest in participating & attending internal development training programs organized by your organization. Organizations have prescheduled development training, programs as refreshers' course for their existing employee, enroll yourself to attend those programs. Don't hesitate to join those quick refresher programs. At times, due to busy work schedule we tend to forget some of the basic key benefits of our product and services. By joining these refresher program either you will learn many new things or you will get chance of revising the key benefits of products and services at a fast pace which can be useful for you in your work and by the help of those key benefits you could also increase your conversion and improve your performance. Apply for some skill development online courses. Learn a new way to complete the same task in more efficient manner. If you'll learn something new, you can present new ideas to your management for approval regarding incorporating a new process or updating an existing process or policy. You will get immediately noticed by showing your interest in improving existing process and policy for benefit of all. Be proactive in asking for a refreshers' training or a short training session on any specific product or services offered by your organization to clarify all your doubts and improve your performance.

By staying away from external negativity

Negativity is a kind of toxic which will corrupts your whole system. Stay away from the negative minded people around you. It will affect your hierarchy and it will keep you negative from inside. There is an excellent example: *Once there was a monkey who was trying to climb a tree and there was another monkey who was not letting him climb the tree by pulling him down through his tail. He tried several times to climb that tree, and unfortunately he couldn't climb it just because of that other monkey. Finally the monkey gave up climbing on that tree and went ahead to the find another tree to climb. Surprisingly from there he quickly climbed the tree.* So the message in it says: stay away from negative minded people from your personal & your professional group because neither they would do it nor they will let others to do it.

By avoiding gossips & commenting on others

Stay away from gossips, it simply passes some irrelevant information from one point to another, if the information is essential then it would be shared by the management across the board and if it's otherwise then there is no point for discussing it and wasting your time.

By making efforts to accomplish your task

First, understand your task thoroughly. Keep in mind that you are the best person that knows what all skills are required to complete your task. Put your smartness with newly learned skills & get desired outcome in a more effective manner. Once you've mastered the art of performing your task in more efficient and effective manner then teach your team members. It will become easy for your team members to adapt your methodology to achieve their targets. In the end you will get recognized not just for mastering the art of performing your duties more efficiently & more effectively but also for helping others (your team members) for achieving their targets or completing their assigned tasks more effectively. This shows your leadership personality and your willingness to grow together as a team.

By helping other team

After mastering your individual task assigned by your immediate supervisor, be proactive to learn a few more new tasks from other team. Ask for cross function training of other divisions (if possible) to help them in time of high work flow or in the event of unavailability of existing staff due to any reason (leave of absence or sickness). This is known as *"cross-functional training"* and it's highly appreciated in the corporate environment. By this, you will be able to do some of the task of other team *(only after completing your personal daily task assigned by your immediate supervisor)* and offer help to other team leader especially when they are working hard on completing some of the time sensitive task with less staff. This will get you noticed before your management and you are also building a good rapport with other team leaders to whom you aren't directly reporting.

By constant learning:

High salary earners don't work only on their job, they work on themself too. When you learn something, it helps you to approach your problems in a different way. Soon you will develop an attitude to quickly find solutions of your problems and grow yourself. By learning new things you can help others as well. Life itself is a long learning experience and you need to keep learning and acquiring new skills, which will help you become a successful person.

By keeping yourself updated with the current affairs, material changes in your industry and finding out ways to overcome any predictable obstacles which could create hindrance or damage your business in any manner, will make you exceptional resource in your organization.

****

"Double your value to the company."

&

Always bring more to the table than you get paid, *"become invaluable."*

****

Changing Mindset

"Develop a passion for learning.
If you do, you will never cease to
grow."
- Anthony J. D'Angelo

Your mindset requires a growth and it must be kept updated regularly. It indicates that your mindset is under your control. It is the primary key to your success. Often people get polluted by negativity around. I am sure you must have heard of this famous saying ***"An empty mind is a devil's workshop."*** So, don't keep your mind empty or busy with non-productive thoughts, instead invest that same time in learning something new, like a new language, a new program or develop a new hobby or learn something for which you are passionate about.

Getting out of stereotype mindset

Stereotype mindset is all around and everywhere. Yes, it's hard to ignore it but we can beat this by being confident and happy satisfied soul. Our parents are the best people to reach out; they are the one who'll always appreciate us even if we're not good enough. The first step we need to take is to change the scenario we have been carrying in our minds for ages. We need to change our minds, our ideologies, and our thought process to make something happen positively. Overcome all those myths that heard so far and believe in yourself and act accordingly.

Ask yourself, your inner soul will answer it.

We all have a hidden superpower in ourselves, and that is our soul which is connected to the divine self. Divine self is what powers you and makes you do wonders. It is the soul light at our core that chooses to incarnate at this point in time. It's ever-aware and has been thinking since you began existing in this lifetime, and since your birth in other lifetimes. Just sit back and think about it, your soul will answer all your questions. Try to know yourself first, find out your hobbies, your goals, and your area of interests and your dislikes. Once you have figured out your interest and goal then just stick to it, it which helps you to perform the work in next level in your interesting area/field only. Then accordingly, choose your career/ employer which gives you an opportunity to explore your personal interest and undoubtedly you'll excel in your professional career.

For all your today's action you will get paid tomorrow.

Everything in this Cosmos has a cycle, like time, seasons, revolutions, ages etc. Karma has a cycle, which results getting back the same what you gave. Whatever you'll give, you'll get it back as a result, and if you'll work today you'll get paid tomorrow. There's no way to get your result right away. You can't get the reactions without any actions. Always invest your time doing fruitful things and remember patience and perseverance are equally important.

Learn additional professional skills.

Once the 11th President and 'The Missile Man' of India **Dr. A.P.J. Abdul Kalam** have said "**I will continuously acquire knowledge**." There's no specific age or limits for studying and learning something new. In today's competitive environment continuously acquiring of a new skill is very essential. Nowadays there's a tough competition in the market, it's getting hard to get promoted in any organization and life as well. Learning additional skills can boost your concentration, confidence and self-esteem. You must keep learning some additional skills throughout your life.

Time management

An efficient management of the most powerful entity of our life is known as **'TIME'** and it is equally important as our life. If you can't manage your time, you can't manage your life and you'll forever be in shambles. It's important to get well organized to manage your time. You must start setting short term and long term goals it allows you to prioritize what you need to accomplish. By effectively managing your time you can do additional work apart from your daily assigned work, let's say if someone in your team has asked you for a favor to help him in preparing his report, you can do that without affecting your daily work. And the most important part of time management is **'STRESS MANAGEMENT'**, you should keep yourself mentally healthy which will help you to handle the stress. Once you have learnt the art of time management then you will get many benefits like less stress & friction and you will be able to acquire greater achievements. By practicing all of these you will organize your daily work easily and will be able to manage some time for your family, friends and for yourself as well.

Develop your interest towards the work.

Interest is the major factor of your mindset. You must keep yourself motivated, and for staying motivated you must rewarding yourself regularly. If any thought tries to break you down, just throw it out of your mind. It will keep you energized and your positivity will boost the energy of your colleagues as well. If you're interested in your work you will put your full strength into it and get the best results but if you're not, then it will keep demotivating you and you will lose the battle. If you know your goals then you won't get distracted from your work. So, most important thing is you must work in your interesting field.

Read books

Books are our humans' best friend. Knowledge matters a lot in this world, if you keep updating your knowledge then it will make you wise and confident.

There are lots of books which will help you to keep your mind strong and motivated.

Some of my favorite inspirational books are:

"Think Out of The Box" by Som Bathla.

"Think and Grow Rich" by Napoleon Hill.

"Switch: How to Change Things When Change Is Hard" by Chip Heath and Dan Heath.

"The Secret" & "The Power" by Rhonda Byrne.

"The Secrets to a Magical Life" by Vikram Khaitan.

You must read these books or similar books for rejuvenation. They will motivate you to achieve your goals. Remember, successful people have their personal library and they constantly read various articles, books, thesis, business, economy, current affairs and increase their knowledge.

Change your approach towards your life

Changing your approach is the best way to get better results. If you are stuck somewhere and think **"I can't",** then try to change your approach towards it. Analyze your way how you are doing that work and write it down; now try finding a solution of that situation with a new approach *(other than what's written earlier)*. Do experiments and explore new ways for yourself and once you find a new approach that has worked for you, then help others by sharing your idea. Try to say '**no**' if you feel that is toxic in your life. Don't accept anything which leads you down.

Overcome the fear of delay

Do your work with honesty and 100% efforts. Try to explore and find some creative ideas from your mind. It might be possible that it will take a bit of extra time but if you are able to secure the expected result (*if you win*) then you will get appreciation from your senior management. Somehow if you fail, you have learnt a lesson and still you have shown your efforts in undertaking a new challenge when other haven't; this will show your positive approach in front of your management. In the end you will get rewarded for your work & extra efforts.

Apply 80-20% rule - "You can't satisfy everyone but you can satisfy and win 80%"

Not every time your idea would get neglected or you'd get bullied for some reasons; 80-20 rule says: Focus on 80% and don't worry about the remaining 20% and always remain positive, enthusiastic and generous while doing your job. It will influence people to talk to you sincerely. Only those, who wouldn't appreciate that you are getting valued only they will be left dissatisfied, ignore them. Don't focus on satisfying someone like: your immediate supervisor, your manager, your leads or fellow team members, instead just work on improving your individual performance and help your team members to achieve their targets too, your efforts gets noticed by the management you'll get a step closer to your promotion and hike.

Attitude is everything

If you want to lead yourself and achieve success then a positive attitude will work for you. You can achieve your goals and success if you have a positive attitude toward your work. Employer's satisfaction depends upon your involvement & commitments. Psychologist **Carol Dweck** has spent her entire career studying attitude and performance, and her latest study shows that *"your attitude is a better predictor of your success than your IQ."* Dweck found that people's core attitudes fall into one of two categories: (i) fixed mindset or (ii) growth mindset. You must try to grow and develop your mindset which will help you to enhance your performance level and goodwill at work.

Keep no room for "EGO"

There's a very thin line between ego and self-respect, often people couldn't differentiate them. Father of the nation **Mahatma Gandhi** stated *"When ego dies, soul awakes."* It means if you want to express the real you then you have to crush your ego, and if it comes on knowledge and personality then you must follow the great scientist Sir Albert Einstein who stated "**More the knowledge, lesser the ego. Lesser the knowledge, more the ego**." Ego makes you think of unnecessary points which are not good for you and your career.

Say a big NO to "OVERCONFIDENCE"

There's old saying that "it's good to be confident but overconfidence is dangerous." It means your overconfidence can harm you. As the first man went on the moon **Neil Armstrong** had stated, *"Well, I think we tried very hard not to be overconfident, because when you get overconfident, that's when something snaps up and bites you."* Overconfidence commonly makes people to do mistakes and lose the grand battles. Stay away from it and stay confident, which will lead you to be one of the best employee of your team or organization.

NEVER compare yourself with others

If you'll waste your time comparing yourself to others, you won't get time to do your work. Sometimes we are fond of comparing ourselves and think about being taller, smarter or fair and those are things which we can't change or develop. So, always think you are amazing in the way you are. Often we see someone doing something amazing and we wish we could do it as well, but it is not the right use of your time. You must focus on your work & self-development that will be fruitful for you.

Take Action

Yes, it will take time to change yourself into an improvised personality, let's say your version **2.0**, but you can start with implementing small changes along the way and slowly & gradually you'd have accomplished many short goals and created your new personality as a most improved professional. Small changes would help you achieve the shorter goals and you will develop a positive mindset upon successfully achieving your shorter goals. Improve your personal development skills for your personal growth which will make you to take action that leads to success.

Set an example for others

Show your skills & orientation without any fear of creating competition, instead you are mastering it by educating your team. Show your tricks and give tips to perform the same task more efficiently. Positively influence your team. Take charge to share your knowledge and experience with new joiners and incubator team members.

Train your junior

Ask management to allow you to train your juniors in your team, which will eventually polish your knowledge and skills as well. Clearing their doubts and educating them about the products & processes will give them confidence in their work and may also bring out creative thoughts and ideas from them.

Start mentoring your juniors; assist them in completing their task.

Improve and make new habits (Apply 21 day rule)

It takes 21 days to develop new habit and then it will become your daily practice. If your vision is to get successful, replace your bad habits with some good ones and in result your life will be changed permanently.

Start with reading articles that interests you.

Reading is an essential hobby. Regular reading makes you smarter and it increases your brain power. Start reading newspapers and choose some of your favorite books. Top billionaires in the world like - ***Warren Buffett & Bill Gates reads 5 hours daily, they read 5 newspapers and corporate documents every single day***. That makes sense, what keeps them calm and sharp is reading and growing.

Observe: (Learn from others)

Observation is a skill that you learn by having patience and zeal to learn something new from others. There are lots of examples from where you can observe and learn things. You can read newspapers - observe what's new and what is important for you in it, you can go to your senior executives and managers of company - observe how they listen to everyone and how they response to each challenge. You can observe their positive approach towards business, professional & personal life. How they manage their work calmly and motivate their teams as well. Learn from seniors, they won't teach you about professional life only, rather they have quite long personal life experience. Go beyond of your thoughts; observe each and every person or thing in order to gain information. It also enhances your ability to interact with others and respond in an appropriate manner. By learning new things and keeping keen observation you'll get clear way to your success.

Give yourself a commitment

Be honest with yourself, the best commitment you can do is giving yourself a commitment of development. Let your desires grow and commit yourself that you'll make them true. It will force you to do and achieve whatever you've committed to yourself and it will make you to succeed anyhow. There could be lot of distractions but if you're committed to complete your task within a given deadline, you'll complete it first. It will increase your self-confidence and encourages you to achieve more.

Finish what you have started

There's a famous book "**Finish What You Start: The Art of Following Through, Taking Action, Executing, & Self-Discipline**" by *Peter Hollins*. He elaborated very finely that how to finish your pending work or study which you had started earlier. Just remember, you have started with a vision and don't let that vision of yours disappear by leaving that task incomplete. Whenever you feel you are disconnected, give yourself a break, ask your conscience and recall your initial vision that has brought you at your current state, now you are just few steps away to transform your vision into a reality. ***Don't give up!***

Don't worry if you are making mistakes, at least you are trying. Remember, mistakes can be corrected but if you don't try, nobody can help you. You can do anything but you can't do everything. So if you have started anything like studies, reading a book, investment plan, etc, then you must do it and complete it. If you have some personal and professional goals, go get them.

Once the founder of Facebook Mark Zuckerberg have said:

*"**Don't be afraid of making mistake but be afraid of not making one**."*

Don't think your task is tough or difficult to it get done, don't assume it that you can't do it, best way is to break it in into small steps and try completing each step one after another and at the end your entire task gets completed. There's nothing impossible that you can't do either you have all the required skills or you don't and if you don't then in that case skills can be learned but if you'll doubt yourself, it wouldn't be easy to complete even an easy task. The best path is to believe in yourself in any situation. Once you'll start finishing your pending work, study and challenges, you will start leading towards your path of successful life.

Advantages of taking new task/challenges:

The moment you take-up a new task as a challenge it will be more interesting to complete that challenge as soon as possible. You are trying a new task *(if challenge is accepted)* under the same employer, so there is no risk of losing your current job. Hence, instead of accepting new task *(challenge)* under the new employer and trying to meet those commitments at same time, you have to build your rapport and show your efficiency and to create a mark for yourself will be challenging and time consuming, wherein. If you accept to undertake new task under same employer, then you don't need to worry about aforesaid concerns.

1) You are existing employee and you have portrait your image before your employer, based on your previous work and your acceptance of a new task.

2) If you succeed, then you will get recognized.

3) Even if you fail, your existing image won't damage.

Overall, you will end up earning more respect that you have accepted new challenges and tasks. Companies encourage their team to open up before them if they wish to undertake any new task without worrying about its outcome as long as the intentions are positive and in favorable to the management and entire company.

Current Scenario

Some people are happy where they are in their current situation. We call it as their "**Comfort Zone**." Although, this comfort zone is good for satisfied souls who don't wish to walk that extra mile to achieve something rewarding. Their mentality is also restricted and revolves around their comfort zone's boundaries. *What about you? Are you happy with the current scenario and your low paycheck? Are you happy with your current position? Since how long you haven't been promoted? When was the last time you have received a decent salary increase?* Your mind will only be happy when you'll be satisfied and feel a sense of accomplishment in your work. If you are happy then only you can work with full concentration and you will get better results. *Are you expecting more from yourself or from your organization?* Speak up and try to find the way which can make this happen. *Have you ever thought that, what you like and how you like to do it? Have you ever imagined becoming a best performer? Doesn't it sound great? Ever thought, what all you need to do to grow your paycheck?*

You are getting paid for

Do you think that you're still not getting paid of what you're worth of? If you see job openings for a similar position like yours with a higher salary that means, you're not getting paid fairly. You're getting paid for your work what you're doing, efforts which you make, results what you deliver and the most important is you're giving your time to your employer. Make it fruitful for your company, your employer and for yourself as well. It's important to justify your work for what you're getting paid for. If you'll keep performing better, then you can ask for a raise.

All that work you have done till date

If you have tried everything and nothing is working out then, you must think about it and write it down. Think about those tasks which you have done till date. Note down your tasks starting from easy task to the toughest one. From a favor for any colleague to some unwanted orders from your boss. Whatever you have done will come back to you with an amazing essence. Make sure there's a lot of positive and result orienting points, and then only you will be considered by your management for giving you some additional responsibilities and eventually growth and raise in your salary.

All of your existing achievements at work

Have you achieved your all targets within the given deadlines? Have you learned anything new for completing your tasks smartly? Have you done anything differently by thinking out the box? However you have performed in the previous year, you are getting paid accordingly. You can analyze your recent efforts and can do better than that. It's all in you. If you believe then you can do your best.

Write down your every single achievement in your organization till now. Start from small points like appreciation from you manager or bosses; be it on your performance or delivering excellence service or on receipt of client appreciation. Working on weekends and week-offs. Profit making tasks which you've done for your team. Also write down all those help & favor you've done for other team member to make them achieve their target or any task. Write down all sort of personal achievements which you've achieved while working in your company.

Zero to Hero

"Change your isolated personality into a reliable resource in your organization."

"Inaction breeds doubt and fear. Action breeds confidence and courage. If you want to conquer fear, do not sit home and think about it. Go out and get busy"
– Dale Carnegie

It would be completely unfair to consider someone *Zero*. Rather, I'd say, *"Change your isolated personality of a silent resource into a reliable resource in your organization*."

Often, it has been observed in many organizations that there exists great performers in the team yet they don't come in the limelight. Ever wondered why? Are they lacking with courage? These silent employees are generating good revenue for the organization and most of the time they achieve their expected targets yet they don't wish to come forward and live in the spotlight. The only reason that I could possibly think of is the fear of accepting new challenges. They are unable to visualize their potential of leading a team or taking new responsibilities in their plate and being accountable for it.

If you are thinking, "*I can't do it*" or "*I can't get success*," or "*I am not a team player*" then please don't disappoint yourself by thinking "*Will I be able to do it?*" or "*Why me*?" rather focus on "*how can I do it*?" First thing you have to do is "***trust yourself***", and make everyone to believe in you until you succeed.

Create your goodwill

You are solely responsible for creating your goodwill. A goodwill is created by one's efforts, approach towards other team members, and how reliable you are in actual time. Improve yourself, your gesture and your attitude towards the work and your team members, managers and other employees as well. Connect with everyone. Appreciate each and every person's efforts. Start offering assistance when required and feel free to them the one in need. Start helping others so that they would like to help you anytime. These few steps will help you gain confidence and trust of others and they will respect you. This is how you can create your own goodwill.

Persistence

Stay tuned and have patience you will get rewarded. As former U.S. President **Calvin Coolidge** said: "*Nothing in the world can take the place of persistence. Talent will not; nothing is more common than unsuccessful people with talent. Genius will not; unrewarded genius is almost a proverb. Education will not; the world is full of educated derelicts. Persistence and determination alone are omnipotent.*"

Remember Newton's 3rd law of Motion: *(Action and reaction are equal and opposite.)*

Remember, Newton's Third Law of Motion states "**For every action there is an equal and opposite reaction**." In physics this always holds true. That's why it's called a "law" in physics. Like if you'll throw a ball into the sky above it will come back down with the same force.

If you apply this law to your workplace then it will allow you to believe that whatever you do, give or however you behave - you'll get back the same. If you're generous and kind to others then they will also treat you in the same way. If you'll help others then they'll help you back. If you will increase the rate of performance you'll get hike and promotion.

Build rapport with other team members

The CEO of Pepsi **Indra Nooyi** said: *"Whatever anybody says or does, assume positive intent. You will be amazed at how your whole approach to a person or problem becomes very different. When you take negative intent, you'll be angry. If you take away that anger and assume positive intent, you will be amazed."* Listen to everyone and take it in positive way never misunderstand anyone by your ego.

It's tough to understand humans and the only way to influence people is to know them. Be someone who understand them and their problems. Sometimes some colleagues or team members can't perform well just because of some personal issues or grudges, which they couldn't share with you just because they might think you can't understand it. Try to connect with them not by your short greetings "hey" or "good morning" be gentle and friendly sometimes by asking "how are you?" Offer them assistance and help when required. Ask your team members and colleagues that do they need any favor or help. These steps will boost your rapport in your organization. You'll be known for your kindness and your performance as well. Even your management will be ready to listen you always.

Bring referrals in your company:

Share your experiences to your family, friends and relatives. Offer them to join your organization. You will get noticed by senior management. You are spreading a message to your friends that you are happy with your organization. You like your team, work environment, process, & management. Feel free to submit your feedback or fill internal surveys, because a company always encourages its staff to open up and share their ideas which will helps in improvement and growth.

You can give feedback on following points:

i) Process improvement

If you think any changes are required in you process then you must share it with the management, they'll look after it and make it convenient for you and for everyone else as well. Pen-down your ideas in this space below before you forgot it.

----

ii) Employee retention

Ask your management to take employees poll regularly. Ask them to take follow ups, meet and have conversations with their employees.

iii) Removing bottlenecks from the process

It is the most common problem of corporate nowadays. You can give feedback for it. While reading this point, if you have come across any spontaneous idea to remove bottleneck from your process, just write it down in the below given space before you forget it.

-----

iv) Simplify some of the difficult task

If there's any possibility to simplify difficult tasks then you must ask for it as soon as possible. If you can think of any better procedure to perform your existing task in more simplified manner, just write it down first below and then implement it to see its results.

---

v) Any other matter related to location, premises, work ethics, & staff attitude, etc.

There is **NO HARM** in giving feedback, regardless it is positive or negative because by this, you will get noticed for bringing it up in front of the management.

Be positive, feedbacks are not meant to burn any bridges between employer & employee, its purpose is to show the challenges faced by entire team or by an individual team member along with preferred solutions to overcome those challenges.

Give positive feedback:

Give constructive (not adverse) feedback in which improvement is sought:

"If you always do what you've always done, you'll always get what you've always got"

– Henry Ford

Show willingness to give more to your organization.

I really feel underutilized in this organization. I have the energy and motivation to achieve much more than I am doing now. To speak frankly, I am targeting a higher salary than what I am getting now. I am not ashamed to say that as we all wish to. I am ambitious and for me the sky is the limit. I don't like to compare myself with my peers as each person has their own strengths, weaknesses and overall contribution." *Make your performance level as high as you can, say this to your management.*

Ask for a Raise

If you feel undervalued or dissatisfied with your pay raise, then you must stand up for yourself and discuss all of your achievements with your employer (manager or you immediate supervisor) and put your expectations before him. Prepare a detailed report of the management's expectation from you along with your actual achievements during that period. If you have achieved or excelled in your performance then you can confidently discuss about your pay raise with your employer. You may discuss in the following manner:

I really appreciate the opportunities you've given me for greater responsibilities, like other employees. I've been getting great results in those areas over the last year and have exceeded the goals we have created. Could we talk about adjusting my salary to reflect this higher level of contribution?"

"I'm hoping we can talk about my salary. It's been a year since my last raise, and I've taken on a number of new responsibilities since then. I'm managing our entire task and was even able to smooth out that long-running issue with the team (mention that issue/concern), which ended up saving us a lot of time in the last few months. I have become an integral member of the team and have developed innovative ways to contribute to the organization. I think things are going really well, and I'd like to talk about increasing my salary to reflect this new work."

Since the organization is mostly interested in productivity result and result is what I am providing, but it is important that my efforts are acknowledged so, that I can give more productive results. I believe I have gone above and beyond the benchmarks which set for my position when I arrived at the organization.

I am confident that you agree with me on the benefits of this achievement and its contribution to the overall results. Having said so, I find it difficult to hide my disappointment with the fact that this accomplishment was not coupled with an adjustment to my pay. I have always given my best and I am always keen to stay on top of my duties and tasks.

Talk about your personal strengths

Eliminate your weakness and take some time to think about your strengths. Read your role models and follow them. Be in discipline and keep patience. Boost your enthusiasm and creativity. Gain trustworthiness and respect. These steps will emphasize your dedication towards your work...

List your personal strengths:

Prepare a list of all your achievements

Write down your accomplishments; maintain a diary to log your achievements. Use action verbs and think about any positive comments you've received from your bosses and colleagues, problems you've dealt with, any honors or awards you've received, and if you've reached or surpassed any targets. If you have worked in a team, what did your team achieve? You were an integral part of the team so any team accomplishments count as yours. By writing your accomplishments will motivate you.

List your achievements:

Check your company's salary review policy before you ask for it

Read your appointment letter and find your company's salary review policy in it. Go through it and read all the clauses mentioned over there. Consult to your seniors about it; they will guide you better by their experience.

Talk professionally

If you're asking for a pay raise to your management, then you have to sound professional. Ask for pay raise on behalf of your performance, skills and experience. Never involve personal matters & reasons for salary hike, because it can ruin your plan to get hike or promotion.

Maintain calm state of mind

Buddha said, "If you will spend some time each day in quiet meditation — simply calm your mind by focusing on your breathing or a simple mantra — you can, over time, tame the monkeys." (Here monkey is stated for your mind) They will grow more peaceful if you lovingly bring them into submission with a consistent practice of meditation. There are some ways to boost your mental statement, Mindfulness Goes Beyond meditation. While meditation can helps you to overcome your stress as well as to become more relaxed and peaceful. Once you start meditating everyday you'll get the benefits of a quiet calm mind. You can work your way towards a greater happiness and fulfillment in your life, by simply tuning into the small things in life. Here are nine ways to boost the quality of your mind, and achieve success in your life.

Breathe deeply.

Take deep breath, whenever you feel heavy. This can help to calm yourself. It will take away your stress and let you focus on your work instantly.

Gratitude

Gratitude is the most important point for your personal development. It will connect you to your team and colleagues. Who will help you out to complete your tough task while enjoying the life? Keeping a gratitude journal will help you to get rid of the stress of the day. It will also maintain peace in your mind to accept, appreciate and to be calm. Gratitude can lead you to win hearts. Which is good for your goodwill and it will attract your management as well.

Say no to time wasting social applications.

You must keep your phone aside while working because mobile phone and the time wasting applications can distract you from your goals. You can also turn off your phone's notifications, as these can be distracting and pull you away from the present moment. Your messages will still be waiting for you there later when you're ready to go through them.

Turn your phone into the silent mode, it can stop each distraction from entering your mind while working or thinking about any solution. If you got some extra time than utilize the time by gaining new ideas to perform better rather not to waste your time by using social media for chatting.

Have a coffee or tea.

A cup of coffee or tea can help you to calm your mind. It will recharge you for the current or next task.

Listen to instrumental music.

Most of the psychologist says music gives peace, which can raise your quality of mind and help you to relax. Music can heal your stress and it will make you calm to handle the pressure. If your mind will be in a peaceful state then you can perform well, this leads you to get success very soon.

Choose tough tasks to complete first

A tough task takes more strength and energy to perform but it's get easier to complete further tasks. If you choose the toughest task first then next task would be easier. This method will keep your interest high toward your work and you will be succeeding in your work.

Share your feelings to your colleagues.

First listen to them what they have to say, then express your feelings and thoughts, it can help you to connect more deeply to the moment by showing appreciation to the people you talk with, in return they will appreciate your efforts and suggest you the best.

Watch motivational videos.

If you're demotivate and don't want to let yourself down then motivational videos could be one of the best way to boost your energy. It will inspire you to awake the inner you and achieve your targets quickly.

Start writing diary.

It won't be hard to maintain a dairy. Writing a diary make sense because you can find your mistakes and wrong decision instantly without taking helps from someone else. Sometimes you'll get answers of the unanswered questions and solutions of unsolved problems. It will make you to manage your work smoothly.

People are so busy focusing on their problems that they forget to find other ways to solve it or get out from it. They get trapped in to the competition, and they forget to enjoy the little things which work even better.

There's a German proverb "***Alles zu seiner zeit***" which means "**all in good time**." Mindfulness will keep reminding you that all good things come with time. It will help you to escape the pressures of your life, and it will make you to enjoy it, and when you will be happy from inside you can work hard and can give your best to achieve all the success what you desire.

1000 Days' Theory

Nowadays it's so easy to switch and find a better job in other companies but as a professional you can stay long in the same organization and keep learning, it will make atmosphere and surrounding's in your favor. There is a principle of corporate sector that if you'll stay 1000 days with the same employer, it will enhance your knowledge, experience and goodwill at your workplace, and when you'll go for a switch even your current employer would try to retrain you in every possible and feasible manner.

Let's say you are working under an employer named ABC corporation and you have completed three years. Your expected annual pay raise will be ranging between 5% to 10% based on your previous year's performance (and 15% in some organization)* so your salary will get increased by 10% i.e., Current Salary + 10% (considering max increase) and let's repeat this calculation for next year assuming you performed well and your salary got increased by additional 10% for 4th year's appraisal i.e., Current Salary + 10% (1st year's increase) + 10% (4th year's increase "if you have worked well in that year as well")and by repeating same calculation. (condition: you have worked well in consecutively for 5th year) for 3 years, your salary will be: Initial Salary + 30% (10*3 considering 10% as each year's appraisal "again considering you were consecutively a good performer in your team and you've worked well all these previous 3 years to consider 10% of increment) and so on for 7th, 8th and 9th year (until you see a reasonably decent raise in your pay or until you get promoted)...

So, in this example, you were able to get your salary raise by 30% after completing 3 years with the same employer by meeting your annual targets and performing well for consecutive 3 years in a row. If you are unable to meet your annual targets or your performance is not up to the mark then you can't expect this 10% salary hike. Whereas, if you change the employer after 3 years (1000 days), you can ask for a minimum of 20%-25% hike on your existing salary and some employers offer even 30% salary growth varies from industry to industry.

Undertake a new responsibility and take a new task every 1000 days. This will give you more exposure to different functionalities and operations and in turn you will learn a complete new task every 1000 days and you learn to master it for another 1000 days and then take up a new task.. If you feel you aren't there yet, you can elevate your performance level right away by bringing in small changes in your daily performance, and before you know it, you're rising up above the sky so high! Slowly and gradually you will take up a new task and learn to master it as well as teach others and then again you take another new task and continue the same process.

Focus and develop your strengths to bring out the best in your work. Knowing the strengths of your coworkers also helps in upgrading the quality of your company's product and services. Your unique skills will not only set you apart from your peers but will also make you an indispensable part of the team and the company. Make sure that you are well acquainted with the nitty-gritty details of your job and company profile. Staying up-to-date with the organization and keep adding task will be a great add-on. So, no one can beat you or stand near you.

If you don't get a new task from your existing employers, you'll end up doing the same monotonous task each year repeatedly. Then it's time to either change the environment or change the employer otherwise you are reducing the pace of your professional growth in that organization.

Hence, by changing your employer not only benefits you in increasing your salary but also gives you exposure to the different work environments. Unfortunately, every industry has a pre-defined benchmark for the salary to be offered irrespective of your skills & experience, although there are exceptions if you are extra-ordinary skilled & talented professional and if you are able to justify your deliverables to your employer, which is not a case for the majority of the professionals. Hence, the majority of the professional unluckily falls into the trap of pre-defined salary structure and faces many rational challenges to level up their salary to his own expectation.

Now, if you work for any employer for consecutive 3 years (365*3=1095 days) you've crossed the 1000 days' bar with your existing employer, you have proved that you are able to perform your existing roles and responsibilities while working for another employer as well across the globe, but you need to be a bit confident. In the reference of the above-stated example, by working under an employer for 1000 days, you have mastered your skills required to perform this job and by using your existing knowledge, skills and judgment you can negotiate your existing salary bar and ask for a decent raise and if that doesn't work, you are confident enough to look for another job with similar job duties with 20-25-30% spike on your existing salary under the current employer. Hence, within this span of 3 years (1000 days) you have gone through all sorts of challenges and you have learned different ways to overcome all those obstacles that act as a bottleneck in your performance. So if you don't receive a decent salary hike due to standard industry practice and pre-defined any organization's in-house policies then you must think of an action plan to grow your salary which may include working for another employer. If you think that you've performed every possible task or undertaken every possible opportunity for growth that could be performed on your existing job profile without affecting your primary roles and responsibilities and still you are not satisfied with you annual salary appraisal then it's time to change your employer.

*Let's see some **pros & cons** of changing your existing employer:*

Pros:

> *1) You are stepping out of your comfort zone.*
>
> *2) You are accepting a new challenge with a new employer.*
>
> *3) You have displayed your confidence to accept a new task.*
>
> *4) You get a chance to work in a new environment.*

5) You will learn the new ways of performing some of the same tasks in different way.

6) You can use your existing knowledge and skills to prove your caliber.

7) You will be promoted.

8) You get a decent hike.

9) You will get to work with new managers, bosses and colleagues.

Cons:

1) You have to work hard to meet your new employers' expectation.

2) You have to win the confidence of your new employer.

3) You have given away your comfort zone and entered into the new work environment.

4) Understanding working culture can be time-consuming.

5) You may fail to deliver the expected results on time.

6) You may fail to prove yourself to your new employer.

Ask this question to yourself: Am I mentally prepared for all of these? Am I ready to accept a new challenge and step out of my comfort zone for my professional development? If your answer is absolute **'YES'**, then I can confidently say that nobody can stop you from becoming a successful corporate professional and simultaneously growing your paycheck.

Conclusion

What is the most amazing feeling for you? Do you want to stay same as you are or do you wish to grow continuously? Your low expectations will never let you to achieve success. Founder of The Walt Disney Company, "Walt Disney" has stated "*All the adversity I've had in my life, all my troubles and obstacles, have strengthened me...You may not realize it when it happens, but a kick in the teeth may be the best thing in the world for you.*" He struggled a lot for his success, he failed several times but every time he learned something new. His failures made him wise and experienced. Nobody is born successful, everyone has to work hard to achieve success, you could become successful at your work and in your life, just by giving your best and keep trying.

Things will change...

Sometimes you need patience to deal with your hassles. There's a French proverb recorded in English in 1545 says "**ROME was not built in a day**." This means that nothing great comes without hard work and dedication. You need to work hard to achieve success in your life. Everything takes time, you should aim for determination in life, success would follow its' path. Keep working hard and invest your efforts today, you'll definitely get profitable returns tomorrow.

Your actions will give you results, for sure.

As I mentioned in Newton's law topic whatever you do you'll get back the same. By showing your willingness to help others and showing your positive approach will get noticed by management. You must discuss about your performance throughout the year. When you clear your employer's expectations and deliver the best results which can be achieved. It will clear your way to your goals and achieve success.

Stay happy, stay blessed and stay focused.

You can't be perfect but you can be excellent, and that excellence will get you rewarded. Plan your day a night before, and prioritize difficult tasks to complete first. Avoid all type of distractions, and keep yourself energetic, keep reminding yourself about your goals. These steps will keep you happy and satisfied with your work.

It's never too late to start something new if you are willing to grow in your career and eventually grow your paycheck and enhance your value then you can achieve your desired position in organization. There are many ways to calm your mind and boost your enthusiasm. Never let yourself down and never stick to negativity.

Life itself is a bundle of challenges, as we grow we get new challenges. We have to tackle the difficulties, defend ourselves from threats, overcome and complete those challenges. This is life, if you can beat up all the challenges of personal life then you can do the same in your professional life too, which will give you strength to complete new challenges. When you achieve success in those new challenges, your success will motivate you to get a raise and get promoted.

"Enjoy your professional life as well, stay positive and keep growing."

Professional Goals

Don't wait for the correct moment, instead let's start from today itself by first writing down your professional goals (both: short term and long term) and then follow these strategies to advance up your professional career and achieve your goals in the near future.

Write your short term professional goals:

Write your Long term professional goals:

Affirmations

Give yourself a commitment to never give-up on your dreams and learning new skills to achieve success in your professional & personal life. List down the skills that you have ever thought to learn but you could not learn it for some reason. By listing it here, you are giving a strong message to your brain that you haven't gave up on your dreams of learning that new skill for which you have been interested since long. Prioritize it decide on which skill you wish to learn first and then excel in that skill by continuous learning.

Skills I am interested to learn first that shall accelerate my professional career are (in order):

1. _____
2. _____
3. _____
4. _____
5. _____
6. _____
7. _____
8. _____
9. _____
10. _____
11. _____

Disclaimer

The content of this book deals with various steps and principles to reach a desirable designation in an organization. All these steps are widely accepted and followed across the world by working professionals in various organizations. With no intention to endorse someone else's learning as the authors own because the author has shared his learning, truths and beliefs based on his personal experience by working in a corporate environment for over 15+ years. The author hereby declares that this book is his own and autonomous work. Although the author has made every effort to ensure that the information & strategies in this book turn out as a beneficial guide to his readers in advancing-up their career. However; the author hereby disclaims any liability to any individual or entity, for any loss, damage, or disruption caused by acts or omissions of the readers, whether such acts or omissions resulted by implementing any strategies either expressed or implied, in this book. Readers are strongly advised not to take any adverse action after reading this book as the author's sole intent is to help their readers to grow in their profession and not to damage/hurt their career in any manner whatsoever. Also, the author has given credits to appropriate parties whose quotes and references were used while writing this book and if anyone has been missed out, it could be merely a bona fide error.

Credits

1. https://www.pinterest.com
2. https://www.keepinspiring.me/famous-quotes
3. https://www.brainyquote.com
4. https://pixabay.com/images/search/quotes
5. https://www.goodreads.com/quotes
6. https://unsplash.com/s/photos/quotes
7. Wikipedia, Google and other web pages.

About the Author

Advocate Swapnil Modi

M.B.A. (HR) and LL.B. (Gold Medalist)

Swapnil Modi is a dynamic & detailed oriented professional with over **15 years** of extensive corporate experience. He has been ranked as **10X STAR PERFORMER** in his professional career with Etech, Inc.

He was honored with the **GOLD MEDAL** for **RANKING FIRST** in Gujarat University **Final LL.B Examination** & he also was honored with the "**SHIELD & CERTIFICATE**" for **RANKING FIRST** in **MOOT COURT COMPETITION** held in Siddharth Law College, Gandhinagar, Gujarat. He holds a **FIRST CLASS** degree in **M.B.A. (HR)** from **NIMS UNIVERSITY**.

He carries abundant experience in **Reviewing / Drafting / Vetting** on all types of agreements and mitigating risk for his clients. He is an expert in maintaining the highest level of quality in operations; ensuring adherence to all the legal parameters and compliances as per the stringent norms.

Key Takeaways:

Write down your Key Takeaways from this book and revisit this page on regular intervals on achieving your goals each time.

1. _____
2. _____
3. _____
4. _____
5. _____
6. _____
7. _____
8. _____
9. _____
10. _____
11. _____

Thanks Note

I would like to thank all the readers for their support by going through this book. I hope this book helps you to increase productivity as well as enhance your professional personality. When I sit down to write about the ideas or insights I want to share here, there's always a consideration in my mind of how this book can benefit my readers. With so many wonderful resources and articles out there sharing great content and ideas, I want to make sure that my readers are happy with their decision to spend some of their quality time here on my book and learning the hacks of enhancing their professional career.

ALL THE BEST,
ADV. SWAPNIL MODI
M.B.A. (HR) and LL.B. (GOLD MEDALIST)